MW01254946

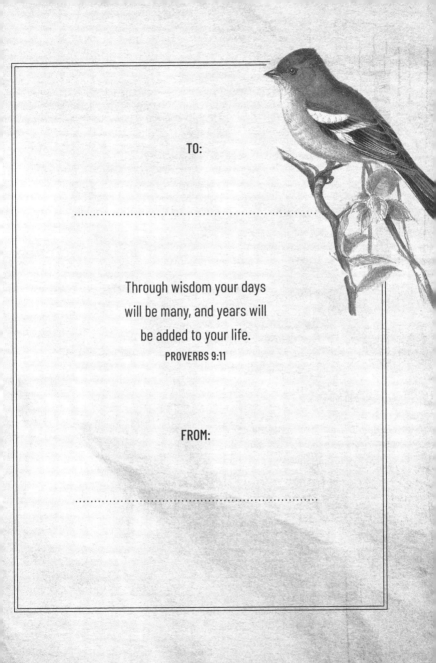

TO:

....

Through wisdom your days
will be many, and years will
be added to your life.
PROVERBS 9:11

FROM:

....

DEVOTIONS FOR
GRANDPAS

ZONDERVAN®

ZONDERVAN

Devotions for Grandpas

© 2025 Zondervan

Published in Grand Rapids, Michigan, by Zondervan. Zondervan is a registered trademark of The Zondervan Corporation, L.L.C., a wholly owned subsidiary of HarperCollins Christian Publishing, Inc.

Requests for information should be addressed to customercare@harpercollins.com.

ISBN 978-0-310-46729-8 (HC)
ISBN 978-0-310-46734-2 (eBook)

Art direction: Gabriella Wikidal

Interior design: Kristy Edwards

Printed in Malaysia

25 26 27 28 29 OFF 10 9 8 7 6 5 4 3 2 1

CONTENTS

May the **FAVOR** of the Lord our
God rest on us; establish the work
of our hands for us—yes, establish
the work of our **HANDS**.

PSALM 90:17

1

WISDOM FOUND

I like the question once asked by Satchel Paige, that venerable alumnus of baseball: "How old would you be if you didn't know how old you were?" An honest answer to that question depends on an honest admission of one's attitude. It has nothing to do with one's age.

The longer I live, the more I become convinced that our major battle in life is not with age but with maturity. There is no choice involved in growing older. God's goal is that we move toward maturity, all our past failures and faults and hang-ups notwithstanding.

Let me leave you three bones to chew on:

1. *Look within and release.* What is it inside you that is stunting your growth? When you find something you are hanging onto too tightly, deliberately let go.
2. *Look around and respond.* Is there some need you can help meet? Risk responding.
3. *Look up and rejoice.* You are the recipient of His riches! And the more involved you remain, the less concern you will have for how old you are.

By the way, how old would you be if you didn't know how old you were?

—CHARLES R. SWINDOLL

GOD'S WORDS FOR YOU, GRANDPA

"Even to your old age and gray hairs I am he, I am he who will sustain you. I have made you and I will carry you; I will sustain you and I will rescue you."

ISAIAH 46:4

They will still bear fruit in old age, they will stay fresh and green, proclaiming, "The Lord is upright; he is my Rock, and there is no wickedness in him."

PSALM 92:14-15

Gray hair is a crown of splendor; it is attained in the way of righteousness.

PROVERBS 16:31

The glory of young men is their strength, gray hair the splendor of the old.

PROVERBS 20:29

He asked you for life, and you gave it to him—length of days, for ever and ever.

PSALM 21:4

Teach us to number our days, that we may gain a heart of wisdom.

PSALM 90:12

The fear of the LORD adds length to life.

PROVERBS 10:27

"With long life I will satisfy him and show him my salvation."

PSALM 91:16

"Is not wisdom found among the aged? Does not long life bring understanding?"

JOB 12:12

"His master replied, 'Well done, good and faithful servant! You have been faithful with a few things; I will put you in charge of many things. Come and share your master's happiness!'"

MATTHEW 25:21

"I have kept the **WAYS** of the LORD;

I am not guilty of turning from my God. . . .

The LORD has rewarded me according

to my **RIGHTEOUSNESS**,

according to my cleanness in his sight.

To the **FAITHFUL** you

show yourself faithful,

to the blameless you show yourself blameless."

2 SAMUEL 22:22, 24–26

2
MORE THAN TODAY

J esus called twelve men to follow Him. Very little is said about what these men left behind, but here were a dozen men who must have wondered about their sanity as they left everything that was comfortable, familiar, and safe to follow Jesus. With laser-beam clarity, the Master had taken aim at their wondering souls.

Choosing to be God's man in your home or in your town may not earn you any immediate or visible commissions. You may experience rejection, alienation, and loneliness because of this decision. There will be times when you wonder if you've done the right thing. But Jesus' promise to you and me is certain: What we see today isn't all there is.

Someday, because of this partnership with our Savior, we will "rejoice . . . and leap for joy" (Luke 6:23). Many people have gone before us; they experienced this same uncertainty, and because they are with their heavenly Father today, their satisfaction is complete . . . for all of eternity.

—ROBERT WOLGEMUTH

GOD'S WORDS FOR YOU, GRANDPA

"The LORD rewards everyone for their righteousness and faithfulness."

1 SAMUEL 26:23

Dear friend, you are faithful in what you are doing for the brothers and sisters, even though they are strangers to you.

3 JOHN V. 5

They could find no corruption in [Daniel], because he was trustworthy and neither corrupt nor negligent.

DANIEL 6:4

A faithful person will be richly blessed.

PROVERBS 28:20

Righteousness and justice are the foundation of your throne; love and faithfulness go before you.

PSALM 89:14

"May the LORD now show you kindness and faithfulness."

2 SAMUEL 2:6

Your love, LORD, reaches to the heavens, your faithfulness to the skies.

PSALM 36:5

I will praise you with the harp for your faithfulness, my God; I will sing praise to you.

PSALM 71:22

LORD, you are my God; I will exalt you and praise your name, for in perfect faithfulness you have done wonderful things, things planned long ago.

ISAIAH 25:1

"I, the LORD, love justice. . . . In my faithfulness I will reward my people and make an everlasting covenant with them."

ISAIAH 61:8

It gave me great joy when some believers came and testified about your faithfulness to the truth, telling how you continue to walk in it.

3 JOHN V. 3

I will bow down toward your holy temple and will praise your name for your unfailing love and your faithfulness, for you have so exalted your solemn decree that it surpasses your fame.

PSALM 138:2

[God] will command his

ANGELS concerning you

to guard you in all your ways. . . .

You will tread on the lion and the cobra;

you will trample the great

LION and the serpent.

"Because he loves me," says the

LORD, "I will rescue him;

I will **PROTECT** him, for he

acknowledges my name."

PSALM 91:11, 13–14

3

THE MOUTHS OF LIONS

Daniel was courageous because he had been obedient to God all along—both in the small things and in the big things. If he hadn't trained himself to obey God every day by always telling the truth, doing his job well, and treating others with kindness, he probably would have buckled when he heard the king's decree not to worship anyone but him. He probably would have thought, *God will understand if I don't pray to Him just this time. It's only for thirty days.*

But Daniel refused to dishonor God. After all, he had seen God rescue Shadrach, Meshach, and Abednego from the fiery furnace. Daniel knew that God cared about him, and he knew that God takes care of His children. So he faced what could have been his death with courage. And how did God repay him? He sent an angel to close those lions' mouths.

The same God who protected Daniel from the lions is working in our lives today. So when trouble strikes, do what Daniel did: "He got down on his knees and prayed, giving thanks to his God, just as he had done before" (Daniel 6:10).

—ROBERT WOLGEMUTH

GOD'S WORDS FOR YOU, GRANDPA

The LORD is my light and my salvation—whom shall I fear? The LORD is the stronghold of my life—of whom shall I be afraid?

PSALM 27:1

The Spirit God gave us does not make us timid, but gives us power.

2 TIMOTHY 1:7

"Do not be dismayed, for I am your God. I will strengthen you and help you."

ISAIAH 41:10

"Do not be afraid, little flock, for your Father has been pleased to give you the kingdom."

LUKE 12:32

When you lie down, you will not be afraid; when you lie down, your sleep will be sweet. Have no fear of sudden disaster or of the ruin that overtakes the wicked, for the LORD will be at your side and will keep your foot from being snared.

PROVERBS 3:24-26

"Be strong and courageous. Do not be afraid; do not be discouraged, for the LORD your God will be with you wherever you go."

JOSHUA 1:9

In righteousness you will be established: Tyranny will be far from you; you will have nothing to fear. Terror will be far removed; it will not come near you.

ISAIAH 54:14

There is no fear in love. But perfect love drives out fear.

1 JOHN 4:18

Though an army besiege me, my heart will not fear; though war break out against me, even then I will be confident.

PSALM 27:3

Even though I walk through the darkest valley, I will fear no evil.

PSALM 23:4

The LORD is with me; I will not be afraid.

PSALM 118:6

When I am afraid, I put my trust in [God].

PSALM 56:3

May these **WORDS** of my mouth

and this meditation of my heart

be **PLEASING** in your sight,

LORD, my Rock and my Redeemer.

PSALM 19:14

4
DAILY CONVERSATIONS

A Christian must transfer ownership of every possession to God. That means his money, time, family, material possessions, education, even earning potential for the future. Doing so is essential to experiencing the Spirit-filled life in his finances.

A Christian must realize that there is absolutely no substitute for this step. If you believe that you are the owner of even a single possession, anything affecting that possession will affect your attitude. God will not input His perfect will into our lives unless we first surrender our will to Him.

If, however, we make a total transfer of everything to God, He will demonstrate His ability. It is important to understand and accept God's conditions for His control (Deuteronomy 5:32–33). God will keep His promise to provide every need we have through physical, material, and spiritual means.

It is simple to say, "I make total transfer of everything to God," but it is not simple to do. At first, it is difficult to consistently seek God's will in the area of material things because we are accustomed to self-management and control. What a great relief it is to turn our burdens over to Him.

—LARRY BURKETT

GOD'S WORDS FOR YOU, GRANDPA

I know what it is to be in need, and I know what is to have plenty.
I have learned the secret of being content in any and every
situation, whether well fed or hungry, whether living in plenty or
in want. I can do all this through him who gives me strength.

PHILIPPIANS 4:12–13

Those who trust in their riches will fall, but the righteous will
thrive like a green leaf.

PROVERBS 11:28

My God will meet all your needs according to the riches of his
glory in Christ Jesus.

PHILIPPIANS 4:19

Lord, you alone are my portion and my cup; you make my lot
secure.

PSALM 16:5

"No one can serve two masters. Either you will hate the one and
love the other, or you will be devoted to the one and despise the
other. You cannot serve both God and money."

MATTHEW 6:24

"Do not worry, saying, 'What shall we eat?' or 'What shall we drink?' or 'What shall we wear?' For the pagans run after all these things, and your heavenly Father knows that you need them. But seek first his kingdom and his righteousness, and all these things will be given to you as well."

MATTHEW 6:31–33

Better the little that the righteous have than the wealth of many wicked.

PSALM 37:16

Whoever loves money never has enough; whoever loves wealth is never satisfied with their income.

ECCLESIASTES 5:10

Whoever gathers money little by little makes it grow.

PROVERBS 13:11

Wisdom is a shelter as money is a shelter, but the advantage of knowledge is this: Wisdom preserves those who have it.

ECCLESIASTES 7:12

These commandments that I give you today are to be on your **HEARTS**. . . . Impress them on your children. **TALK** about them when you sit at home and when you walk along the road, when you lie down and when you get up.

DEUTERONOMY 6:6–7

5

EVERYWHERE IN BETWEEN

Someone coined a phrase to describe how the early church in Jerusalem went about spreading the gospel. It was called "gossiping the gospel"—integrating the gospel into everyday conversation. There were no tracts, books, or Bibles to hand out. Rather, witnessing was a matter of word of mouth wherever people went.

That idea is found in Deuteronomy 6:4–9 where Moses instructed parents on how to pass on the requirements of the covenant, the details of God's law, to their children. He said to talk to the children in the house and in the street, when you're going to bed and when you rise up—and everywhere in between. It was a common Hebrew way of expressing the idea of totality—the two ends of the spectrum included everything in between. But it didn't mean simply to teach children the contents of the covenant. It meant to illustrate how the covenant applied to daily life—in the home, in the street, in the market, and "everywhere in between."

How often in a day do you grasp the opportunity to integrate God's truth into your daily conversations—especially with those who are not believers?

—DR. DAVID JEREMIAH

GOD'S WORDS FOR YOU, GRANDPA

[Paul] traveled through that area, speaking many words of encouragement to the people.

ACTS 20:2

Be wise in the way you act toward outsiders; make the most of every opportunity.

COLOSSIANS 4:5

Do not let any unwholesome talk come out of your mouths, but only what is helpful for building others up according to their needs, that it may benefit those who listen.

EPHESIANS 4:29

My mouth will speak words of wisdom.

PSALM 49:3

The prudent hold their tongues.

PROVERBS 10:19

Speaking the truth in love, we will grow to become in every respect the mature body of him who is the head, that is, Christ.

EPHESIANS 4:15

Put off falsehood and speak truthfully to your neighbor.
 EPHESIANS 4:25

Let your conversation be always full of grace, seasoned with salt,
so that you may know how to answer everyone.
COLOSSIANS 4:6

The lips of the righteous nourish many. . . .
From the mouth of the righteous comes the fruit of wisdom.
PROVERBS 10:21, 31

The mouths of the righteous utter wisdom,
    and their tongues speak what is just.
PSALM 37:30

Be filled with the Spirit, speaking to one another with psalms,
hymns, and songs from the Spirit.
EPHESIANS 5:18–19

The words of the mouth are deep waters,
    but the fountain of wisdom is a rushing stream.
PROVERBS 18:4

"A good man brings good things out of the good stored up in his
heart. . . . For the mouth speaks what the heart is full of."
LUKE 6:45

Have **COMPASSION**

on your servants.

Satisfy us in the morning

with your unfailing **LOVE**,

that we may sing for joy

and be glad all our days.

PSALM 90:13-14

6

COMPASSIONATE LOVE

The truly loving person hands out compassion in free and generous doses. God likens true compassion to a father's empathy for his child. This could also be applied to a grandfather. Who will rise in the middle of the night to hold a grandchild with a fever? Who will run back to the store to pick up one more item for a grandchild's school project? Who will reinforce discipline by firmly adhering to an unpopular restriction?

A grandfather whose heart is filled with compassion.

God shows His compassion to us in that He sent Christ to die for us while we were still sinners (Romans 5:8). God nurses our wounds even though He isn't the one who caused them. When our bodies drag and our spirits sag, it takes a heart committed to God and the infiltrating power of His Holy Spirit to be compassionate. It takes God—with the heart of a grandfather—to bring compassion to those who need it.

Lean into the compassionate love of God. Sigh. Rest.

Then offer what you've been given—freely, lavishly—to those around you.

—ELISA MORGAN

GOD'S WORDS FOR YOU, GRANDPA

"The LORD your God is gracious and compassionate. He will not turn his face from you if you return to him."

2 CHRONICLES 30:9

The LORD is good to all; he has compassion on all he has made.

PSALM 145:9

Praise the LORD, my soul, . . . who redeems your life from the pit and crowns you with love and compassion, who satisfies your desires with good things so that your youth is renewed like the eagle's.

PSALM 103:2, 4–5

The LORD longs to be gracious to you; therefore he will rise up to show you compassion.

ISAIAH 30:18

Praise be to the God and Father of our Lord Jesus Christ, the Father of compassion. . . . Our comfort abounds through Christ.

2 CORINTHIANS 1:3, 5

"He who has compassion on them will guide them and lead them beside springs of water. . . . For the LORD comforts his people and will have compassion on his afflicted ones."

ISAIAH 49:10, 13

"On the day when I act," says the LORD Almighty, "they will be my treasured possession. I will spare them, just as a father has compassion and spares his son who serves him."

MALACHI 3:17

Jesus had compassion on them and touched their eyes. Immediately they received their sight and followed him.

MATTHEW 20:34

Return to the LORD your God,
for he is gracious and compassionate,
slow to anger and abounding in love,
and he relents from sending calamity.

JOEL 2:13

"You will not have to fight this battle. Take up your positions; stand firm and see the deliverance the LORD will give you. . . . Do not be afraid; do not be discouraged."

2 CHRONICLES 20:17

Two are **BETTER** than one,

because they have a good return for their labor:

If either of them falls down,

one can **HELP** the other up. . . .

Also, if two lie down together,

they will keep **WARM**. . . .

A **CORD** of three strands

is not quickly broken.

ECCLESIASTES 4:9-12

7
CHOOSE WISELY

Jesus tells us to love everyone, even our enemies (Luke 6:27, 35). But Proverbs 13:20 says that if we are to grow wise, we must walk with wise people. If we choose "fools" as companions, we'll suffer harm.

A "companion" is much more than an acquaintance; he or she is one who becomes a close friend, a traveling buddy, even a mate. If we choose companions who don't love God or don't act according to His Word, we're told in no uncertain terms that we're walking straight into trouble.

As grandfathers, we know our job is to protect our grandchildren from harm. Therefore our job is to teach them to choose friends wisely. And this lesson is every bit as important for us as it is for our grandkids. Our companions are either making us wiser or leading us right into harm's way.

The Bible doesn't contradict itself at all on this issue. Love your neighbor. Love your enemy. But choose your friends with care.

—ROBERT WOLGEMUTH

GOD'S WORDS FOR YOU, GRANDPA

One who has unreliable friends soon comes to ruin, but there is a friend who sticks closer than a brother.

PROVERBS 18:24

Perfume and incense bring joy to the heart, and the pleasantness of a friend springs from their heartfelt advice.

PROVERBS 27:9

Be devoted to one another in love. Honor one another above yourselves.

ROMANS 12:10

If we walk in the light, as he is in the light, we have fellowship with one another.

1 JOHN 1:7

"Anyone who withholds kindness from a friend forsakes the fear of the Almighty."

JOB 6:14

"Greater love has no one than this: to lay down one's life for one's friends. You are my friends if you do what I command. I no longer call you servants, because a servant does not know his master's business. Instead, I have called you friends."

JOHN 15:13-15

A friend loves at all times, and a brother is born for a time of adversity.

PROVERBS 17:17

"My intercessor is my friend as my eyes pour out tears to God."

JOB 16:20

Let no debt remain outstanding, except the continuing debt to love one another.

ROMANS 13:8

Be perfectly united in mind and thought.

1 CORINTHIANS 1:10

One who loves a pure heart and who speaks with grace will have the king for a friend.

PROVERBS 22:11

God said, "Let us make **MANKIND**

in our image, in our likeness, so that

they may rule over . . . all the creatures

that move along the ground."

So God created mankind in his own **IMAGE**,

in the image of God he created them;

male and female he **CREATED** them.

GENESIS 1:26–27

8
ONLY YOU

There is one area of my life—and yours—in which there is no need for competition. This truth comes through clearly in the words of Jeremiah's call: "Before you were born I set you apart" (Jeremiah 1:5). In other words, God was saying to this prophet, "You're one of a kind, Jeremiah. I have no templates, no stencils. You can look around all you want, but you're the only man who is just like you."

Please do not miss this spellbinding truth: There is no competition in God's plan for you and me. His calling is as individualized as each person's fingerprint; it belongs to no one else.

Does this mean that before my parents had ever met, God had a specific work for me to accomplish? Yes, it does. And does this mean that if I want to discover the greatest joy in living, I need to take my focus away from others and tenaciously seek God's singular direction for me? Again, the answer is in the affirmative.

What has God called you to? Whatever it is, it's all yours. There's no winning or losing in this game . . . there's only obedience.

—ROBERT WOLGEMUTH

GOD'S WORDS FOR YOU, GRANDPA

You created my inmost being; you knit me together in my mother's womb. I praise you because I am fearfully and wonderfully made; your works are wonderful, I know that full well.

PSALM 139:13-14

"Before I formed you in the womb I knew you, before you were born I set you apart."

JEREMIAH 1:5

Do you not know that your bodies are temples of the Holy Spirit, who is in you, whom you have received from God? You are not your own; you were bought at a price. Therefore honor God with your bodies.

1 CORINTHIANS 6:19-20

Wisdom is a shelter as money is a shelter, but the advantage of knowledge is this: Wisdom preserves those who have it.

ECCLESIASTES 7:12

Command those who are rich in this present world not to be arrogant nor to put their hope in wealth, which is so uncertain, but to put their hope in God, who richly provides us with everything for our enjoyment. Command them to do good, to be rich in good deeds, and to be generous and willing to share. In this way they will lay up treasure for themselves as a firm foundation for the coming age, so that they may take hold of the life that is truly life.

1 TIMOTHY 6:17–19

"Where you go I will go, and where you stay I will stay. Your people will be my people and your God my God. Where you die I will die, and there I will be buried. May the LORD deal with me, be it ever so severely, if even death separates you and me."

RUTH 1:16–17

The boundary lines have fallen

for me in **PLEASANT** places;

surely I have a delightful

INHERITANCE.

PSALM 16:6

9

LIVES OF INCREASING

It is not without significance that Paul said, "*I have learned* to be content whatever the circumstances" (Philippians 4:11, italics added). He did not say, "I have always been content with any circumstances." For him, as it will be for us, it had been a painful learning process. The point is that he graduated!

Our Lord likened the Christian life to a river that broadened as it flowed down to the sea—an encouraging picture for the aging Christian. There is no reason why our lives now should not be as enjoyable, stimulating, and fruitful as they were earlier. Lives of increasing instead of diminishing, lives of continual outflow, can be ours.

Read again Christ's alluring picture: "Whoever believes in me, as Scripture has said, rivers of living water will flow from within them" (John 7:38). Such people refuse to concede defeat to Father Time. They resolve to master old age, not be defeated by it. They are grateful, thoughtful, cheerful, and content. Their very resilience is a great encouragement to their contemporaries who are incited to discover their secret.

—J. Oswald Sanders

GOD'S WORDS FOR YOU, GRANDPA

Better a small serving of vegetables with love than a fattened calf with hatred.

PROVERBS 15:17

Each person should live as a believer in whatever situation the Lord has assigned to them, just as God has called them.

1 CORINTHIANS 7:17

Godliness with contentment is great gain. For we brought nothing into the world, and we can take nothing out of it. But if we have food and clothing, we will be content with that.

1 TIMOTHY 6:6-8

Go, eat your food with gladness, and drink your wine with a joyful heart, for God has already approved what you do.

ECCLESIASTES 9:7

The cheerful heart has a continual feast.

PROVERBS 15:15

Better one handful with tranquility than two handfuls with toil and chasing after the wind.

ECCLESIASTES 4:6

A happy heart makes the face cheerful.

PROVERBS 15:13

Give me neither poverty nor riches, but give me only my daily bread.

PROVERBS 30:8

Better a little with the fear of the LORD than great wealth with turmoil.

PROVERBS 15:16

Better a little with righteousness than much gain with injustice.

PROVERBS 16:8

Better a dry crust with peace and quiet than a house full of feasting, with strife.

PROVERBS 17:1

God is our **REFUGE** and strength,

an ever-present help in trouble.

Therefore we will not fear,

though the **EARTH** give way

and the mountains fall into

the **HEART** of the sea,

though its waters roar and foam

and the mountains **QUAKE**

with their surging.

PSALM 46:1-3

10
SAME LAND, SAME GIANTS

Discouragement and disappointment are like twins. Open the door to disappointment, and you will find discouragement close behind. Satan's goal is to dishearten you. Once discouragement enters your camp, it seems to be downhill all the way.

That's why God was careful in His instructions to Joshua as the Israelites prepared to occupy the land God had given them. They had missed occupying Canaan because of unbelief at Kadesh Barnea. Some forty years later, they were preparing to enter the same land and meet the same giants. So God said, not once but three times, "Be strong and courageous" (Joshua 1:6, 7, 9)! Yet they would not listen. Word of the giants and the fortified cities had penetrated their line of defense. Discouragement followed, bringing dejection and despair, until they were totally demoralized.

What is God's word to you today? It is to be strong and courageous, for your Father, the Lord God Omnipotent, reigns. Stop weeping and rejoice in the God of your salvation. He is your strength and He will enable you to stand (Habakkuk 3:18–19).

—KAY ARTHUR

GOD'S WORDS FOR YOU, GRANDPA

Wait for the LORD; be strong and take heart and wait for the LORD.

PSALM 27:14

Strengthen the feeble hands, steady the knees that give way; say to those with fearful hearts, "Be strong, do not fear; your God will come."

ISAIAH 35:3–4

Because the hand of the LORD my God was on me, I took courage.

EZRA 7:28

"The LORD himself goes before you and will be with you; he will never leave you nor forsake you. Do not be afraid; do not be discouraged."

DEUTERONOMY 31:8

"Be strong and courageous, and do the work. Do not be afraid or discouraged, for the LORD God, my God, is with you. He will not fail you or forsake you."

1 CHRONICLES 28:20

Though I have fallen, I will rise. Though I sit in darkness, the Lord will be my light.

MICAH 7:8

The Lord is good to those whose hope is in him, to the one who seeks him.

LAMENTATIONS 3:25

I sought the Lord, and he answered me; he delivered me from all my fears.

PSALM 34:4

"I have **TOLD** you these things, so that in me you may have **PEACE**. In this world you will have trouble. But take **HEART**! I have overcome the world."

JOHN 16:33

11

COME OPENLY TO HIM

It is one thing to feel loved by God when our life is together and all our support systems are in place. But what happens when we sin and fail, when our dreams shatter, when our investments crash, when we are regarded with suspicion? What happens when we come face-to-face with the human condition?

God calls us to come openly to Him. God is the Father who ran to His prodigal son when he came limping home. God loves who we really are—whether we like it or not. God calls us, as He did Adam (Genesis 3:8–9), to come out of hiding. No amount of spiritual makeup can render us more presentable to Him.

"Come to Me now," Jesus says. "Acknowledge and accept who I want to be for you: a Savior of boundless compassion, infinite patience, unbearable forgiveness, and love that keeps no score of wrongs. Quit projecting onto Me your own feelings about yourself. At this moment your life is a bruised reed and I will not crush it, a smoldering wick and I will not quench it. You are in a safe place."

—BRENNAN MANNING

Just as we share abundantly in the sufferings of Christ, so also our comfort abounds through Christ.

2 CORINTHIANS 1:5

Our present sufferings are not worth comparing with the glory that will be revealed in us.

ROMANS 8:18

We also glory in our sufferings, because we know that suffering produces perseverance; perseverance, character; and character, hope.

ROMANS 5:3-4

Consider it pure joy, my brothers and sisters, whenever you face trials of many kinds, because you know that the testing of your faith produces perseverance.

JAMES 1:2-3

The righteous person may have many troubles, but the LORD delivers him from them all.

PSALM 34:19

For Christ's sake, I delight in weaknesses, in insults, in hardships, in persecutions, in difficulties. For when I am weak, then I am strong.

2 CORINTHIANS 12:10

Blessed is the one who perseveres under trial because, having stood the test, that person will receive the crown of life that the Lord has promised to those who love him.

JAMES 1:12

You have been a refuge for the poor, a refuge for the needy in their distress, a shelter from the storm and a shade from the heat.

ISAIAH 25:4

The Spirit helps us in our weakness. We do not know what we ought to pray for, but the Spirit himself intercedes for us through wordless groans.

ROMANS 8:26

In the day of trouble he will keep me safe in his dwelling; he will hide me in the shelter of his sacred tent and set me high upon a rock.

PSALM 27:5

Whatever you do, work at it with all your heart, as working for the Lord, not for human masters, since you know that you will receive an inheritance from the Lord as a **REWARD**. It is the Lord Christ you are serving.

COLOSSIANS 3:23–24

12
LIGHT OF DAY

The apostle Paul declared, "I strive always to keep my conscience clear before God and man" (Acts 24:16). Imagine the courage, confidence, and self-assurance it took to say such a thing in the face of one's accusers.

What does it mean to have a clear conscience? It means that you can say with a straight face, "I have done everything I can do. There are no sins to confess. Look wherever you want, but there will be no surprises."

We are living in a time when men are quietly scrambling to hide from their pasts. Every day we hear of yet another man whose treacherous history is brought into the light of day.

Where are the Pauls? Where are the men who live with clear consciences? Do we live our lives just one small step ahead of the truth of our pasts, or do we rest because we've withheld no secrets?

You may have some confessions to submit, a record to clear up. There could be consequences. But my guess is that Paul would promise us that a soul vindicated from full disclosure is well worth any price we may have to pay. Regardless of the cost, it'll be worth it.

—Robert Wolgemuth

GOD'S WORDS FOR YOU, GRANDPA

The LORD . . . delights in people who are trustworthy.
PROVERBS 12:22

To do what is right and just is more acceptable to the LORD than sacrifice.
PROVERBS 21:3

The integrity of the upright guides them, but the unfaithful are destroyed by their duplicity.
PROVERBS 11:3

Whoever walks in integrity walks securely, but whoever takes crooked paths will be found out.
PROVERBS 10:9

Make it your ambition to lead a quiet life: You should mind your own business and work with your hands, . . . so that your daily life may win the respect of outsiders and so that you will not be dependent on anybody.
1 THESSALONIANS 4:11–12

Live such good lives among [unbelievers] that, though they accuse you of doing wrong, they may see your good deeds and glorify God on the day he visits us.

1 PETER 2:12

Let the LORD judge the peoples. Vindicate me, LORD, according to my righteousness, according to my integrity, O Most High.

PSALM 7:8

He has shown you, O mortal, what is good. And what does the LORD require of you? To act justly and to love mercy and to walk humbly with your God.

MICAH 6:8

Righteousness guards the person of integrity.

PROVERBS 13:6

May integrity and uprightness protect me, because my hope, LORD, is in you.

PSALM 25:21

The LORD . . . takes the upright into his confidence.

PROVERBS 3:32

"When you **PASS** through the waters,

I will be with you;

and when you pass through the **RIVERS**,

they will not sweep over you.

When you **WALK** through the fire,

you will not be burned;

the **FLAMES** will not set you ablaze."

ISAIAH 43:2

13

THE ROLE OF THE NURTURER

I f you desire to influence another person, the way to start is by nurturing them. What clergyman John Knox said over four hundred years ago is still true: "You cannot antagonize and influence at the same time."

At the heart of the nurturing process is genuine concern for others. And as we try to help and influence the people around us, we must have positive feelings and concern for them. If you want to help people and make a positive impact on them, you cannot dislike or disparage them. You must give love to them and give them respect.

You may be wondering why you should take on a nurturing role with the people you want to influence, especially if they are employees, colleagues, or friends. You may be saying to yourself, "Isn't that something they can get somewhere else, like at home?" The unfortunate truth is that most people are desperate for encouragement. If you become a major nurturer in the life of another person, then you have an opportunity to make a major impact on them.

—JOHN MAXWELL

GOD'S WORDS FOR YOU, GRANDPA

Cast your cares on the LORD and he will sustain you; he will never let the righteous be shaken.

PSALM 55:22

In my alarm I said, "I am cut off from your sight!" Yet you heard my cry for mercy when I called to you for help.

PSALM 31:22

Truly my soul finds rest in God; my salvation comes from him.

PSALM 62:1

My soul is downcast within me. Yet this I call to mind and therefore I have hope: Because of the LORD's great love we are not consumed, for his compassions never fail. They are new every morning; great is your faithfulness.

LAMENTATIONS 3:20–23

Let the morning bring me word of your unfailing love, for I have put my trust in you. Show me the way I should go, for to you I entrust my life.

PSALM 143:8

My flesh and my heart may fail, but God is the strength of my heart and my portion forever.

PSALM 73:26

"I am the LORD your God who takes hold of your right hand and says to you, Do not fear; I will help you."

ISAIAH 41:13

He will show compassion, so great is his unfailing love.

LAMENTATIONS 3:32

In all their distress [the Lord] too was distressed, and the angel of his presence saved them. In his love and mercy he redeemed them; he lifted them up and carried them all the days of old.

ISAIAH 63:9

"I will refresh the weary and satisfy the faint."

JEREMIAH 31:25

"Let us **ACKNOWLEDGE** the LORD;

let us press on to acknowledge him.

As surely as the **SUN** rises,

he will appear;

he will come to us like the

WINTER rains."

HOSEA 6:3

14

A NEW STEP OF FAITH

Y ou must admit, it was some kind of unorthodox military strategy: March around the city for six days without saying a word, on the seventh day go around seven times, listen for the long blast of the trumpet, and then shout.

Not exactly your ordinary procedure, but Joshua heard it in striking fashion from the commander of the Lord's army (Joshua 5:14), and he in turn passed it on to the people.

The Israelites followed God's instructions to a tee, even though the whole operation was a venture of faith that involved taking a tremendous risk. In the face of insurmountable odds, they relied on God's faithfulness. A nation notorious for its murmuring and complaining obeyed in silence. What a testimony to God's power.

Do you today face a personal Jericho—some unanswered prayer for family members or friends, some seemingly hopeless situation? Perhaps God is calling you today to a new step of faith, to a new risk-taking! The story of God's victory at Jericho rules out any hint of fatalism, which gives up hope because of high walls. It is God Himself who brings down the walls.

—DIRK R. BUURSMA

GOD'S WORDS FOR YOU, GRANDPA

Faith is confidence in what we hope for and assurance about what we do not see.

HEBREWS 11:1

Faith comes from hearing the message, and the message is heard through the word about Christ.

ROMANS 10:17

Abram believed the LORD, and he credited it to him as righteousness.

GENESIS 15:6

"Truly I tell you, if you have faith as small as a mustard seed, you can say to this mountain, 'Move from here to there,' and it will move. Nothing will be impossible for you."

MATTHEW 17:20

By faith we understand that the universe was formed at God's command, so that what is seen was not made out of what was visible.

HEBREWS 11:3

We live by faith, not by sight.

2 CORINTHIANS 5:7

It is by grace you have been saved, through faith—and this is not from yourselves, it is the gift of God—not by works, so that no one can boast.

EPHESIANS 2:8-9

Since we have been justified through faith, we have peace with God through our Lord Jesus Christ.

ROMANS 5:1

This righteousness is given through faith in Jesus Christ to all who believe.

ROMANS 3:22

The promise [of salvation] comes by faith, so that it may be by grace and may be guaranteed.

ROMANS 4:16

God has given us eternal life, and this life is in his Son. Whoever has the Son has life.

1 JOHN 5:11-12

From **EVERLASTING** to everlasting

the LORD's love is with those

who fear him,

and his **RIGHTEOUSNESS**

with their children's children.

PSALM 103:17

15

THE SOLIDARITY
OF FAMILY

God loves older people, and He has created them with inherent dignity. But another side of the dignity and worth of old age comes more specifically from a Christian understanding of the world. Christians understand the existence of another world, the world of God's love, toward which or against which our lives are being shaped. If you believe in this other world, it is not very hard to see that old age is meant to prepare us for it. So much that will be valueless there becomes, already, valueless here—independence, pride, wealth. So much that the kingdom of love depends on becomes already vitally necessary—interdependence, kindness, humility.

These qualities are usually expressed in families. To a remarkable degree, children and other relatives do get involved. While other relationships may shrivel to almost nothing, family relationships often grow stronger.

In that interlocking of parents and children, part of the goodness of old age reveals itself. You see the solidarity of human beings of all ages, a solidarity expressed concretely by the family. We really are in this together.

—Tim Stafford

GOD'S WORDS FOR YOU, GRANDPA

"A man will leave his father and mother and be united to his wife, and the two will become one flesh."

EPHESIANS 5:31

All your children will be taught by the LORD, and great will be their peace.

ISAIAH 54:13

"Whatever you did for one of the least of these brothers and sisters of mine, you did for me."

MATTHEW 25:40

As we have opportunity, let us do good to all people, especially to those who belong to the family of believers.

GALATIANS 6:10

If we walk in the light, as he is in the light, we have fellowship with one another, and the blood of Jesus, his Son, purifies us from all sin. . . . If we confess our sins, he is faithful and just and will forgive us our sins and purify us from all unrighteousness.

1 JOHN 1:7, 9

Both the one who makes people holy and those who are made
holy are of the same family. So Jesus is not ashamed to call them
brothers and sisters.
HEBREWS 2:11

When you were dead in your sins and in the uncircumcision of
your flesh, God made you alive with Christ. He forgave us all our
sins, having canceled the charge of our legal indebtedness, which
stood against us and condemned us; he has taken it away, nailing
it to the cross.
COLOSSIANS 2:13–14

He has rescued us from the dominion of darkness and brought
us into the kingdom of the Son he loves, in whom we have
redemption, the forgiveness of sins.
COLOSSIANS 1:13–14

The Lord our God is merciful and forgiving, even though we have
rebelled against him.
DANIEL 9:9

Who is a God like you, who pardons sin and forgives the
transgression of the remnant of his inheritance? You do not stay
angry forever but delight to show mercy.
MICAH 7:18

Lord, hear my voice.

Let your ears be attentive

to my cry for **MERCY**.

If you, LORD, kept a record of sins,

Lord, who could stand?

But with you there is **FORGIVENESS**. . . .

I wait for the LORD . . . and in his

WORD I put my hope.

PSALM 130:2-5

16

THE BASIS OF LOVE

Tears came to her eyes as she read the letter. It was from a friend of her son, yes, her son who had run out of her life so many years ago. Abandoned her.

Her son's friend told how her son had been pursued and captured by the Lord, the same Lord who had changed her life. He wanted to come back now, to make it right again. In fact, he was coming back today. Today!

The pain he's put me through. I just don't know if I can forgive him. I want him to feel my pain and keep on feeling it all the days of his life. Why should I forgive him? He doesn't deserve it!

There was a knock at the door. Trembling with emotion, she opened it. The face—she had not seen the face for so long. The memories of rejection, pain, despair came flooding back. Then she remembered the letter she had just read: "I appeal to you on the basis of love . . . welcome him."

O Lord, I just don't know if I can forgive him. Please forgive me, Lord, forgive me. And at that moment, in the power of feeling forgiven, she reached out her arms—and welcomed him back.

—Dirk R. Buursma

As far as the east is from the west, so far has he removed our transgressions from us.

PSALM 103:12

"I will cleanse them from all the sin they have committed against me and will forgive all their sins of rebellion against me."

JEREMIAH 33:8

Bear with each other and forgive one another if any of you has a grievance against someone. Forgive as the Lord forgave you.

COLOSSIANS 3:13

In him we have redemption through his blood, the forgiveness of sins, in accordance with the riches of God's grace that he lavished on us.

EPHESIANS 1:7-8

God was reconciling the world to himself in Christ, not counting people's sins against them. And he has committed to us the message of reconciliation.

2 CORINTHIANS 5:19

He has reconciled you by Christ's physical body through death to present you holy in his sight, without blemish and free from accusation.

COLOSSIANS 1:22

Blessed is the one whose transgressions are forgiven, whose sins are covered. Blessed is the one whose sin the LORD does not count against them and in whose spirit is no deceit.

PSALM 32:1-2

Peter came to Jesus and asked, "Lord, how many times shall I forgive my brother or sister who sins against me? Up to seven times?" Jesus answered, "I tell you, not seven times, but seventy-seven times."

MATTHEW 18:21-22

There is now no condemnation for those who are in Christ Jesus.

ROMANS 8:1

Be kind and compassionate to one another, forgiving each other, just as in Christ God forgave you.

EPHESIANS 4:32

If anyone has **MATERIAL** possessions and sees a brother or sister in need but has no pity on them, how can the **LOVE** of God be in that person? Dear children, let us not love with words or speech but with **ACTIONS** and in truth.

1 JOHN 3:17–18

17

COMPASSIONATE REWARD

Have you ever tried to sympathize with a grandchild who's suffered a scuffed knee without squatting down and stooping to his or her level? Of course such a thing is impossible. Unless a child sees the understanding on your face and sees it down on his or her level, that child won't be able to accept your comfort.

The psalmist David saw that God demonstrated this kind of care for His children. David called it "compassion": "Praise the LORD ... who forgives all your sins and heals all your diseases" (Psalm 103:2–3). God the Father takes moments from His busy schedule—keeping the stars and planets on their charted courses, growing food for a hungry world, raising up and bringing down world leaders—to stoop to our level and have compassion on His bumped and bruised children.

You're a busy man. But our busy heavenly Father, the Creator of the universe, has compassion. He's never too busy to stop, never too proud to stoop. It's a good thing too. How else could we ever see His face?

Look carefully—this Father's got lots of love. He stops, then He stoops. I guess if He can do it, so can we.

—ROBERT WOLGEMUTH

Good will come to those who are generous and lend freely, who conduct their affairs with justice.

PSALM 112:5

Blessed is the one who is kind to the needy.

PROVERBS 14:21

Love is kind.

1 CORINTHIANS 13:4

Carry each other's burdens, and in this way you will fulfill the law of Christ.

GALATIANS 6:2

We are taking pains to do what is right, not only in the eyes of the Lord but also in the eyes of man.

2 CORINTHIANS 8:21

When the kindness and love of God our Savior appeared, he saved us, not because of righteous things we had done, but because of his mercy.

TITUS 3:4–5

"Come, you who are blessed by my Father; take your inheritance, the kingdom prepared for you since the creation of the world. For I was hungry and you gave me something to eat, I was thirsty and you gave me something to drink, I was a stranger and you invited me in, I needed clothes and you clothed me, I was sick and you looked after me, I was in prison and you came to visit me."

MATTHEW 25:34–36

As we have opportunity, let us do good to all people.

GALATIANS 6:10

As God's chosen people, holy and dearly loved, clothe yourselves with compassion, kindness, humility, gentleness and patience.

COLOSSIANS 3:12

The fruit of the Spirit is love, joy, peace, forbearance, kindness, goodness, faithfulness, gentleness and self-control.

GALATIANS 5:22–23

"If anyone gives even a cup of cold water to one of these little ones who is my disciple, truly I tell you, that person will certainly not lose their reward."

MATTHEW 10:42

"For I know the **PLANS** I have for

you," declares the LORD, "plans to

PROSPER you and not to harm you,

plans to give you **HOPE** and a future."

JEREMIAH 29:11

18

SAFELY IN GOD'S PRESENCE

The Bible tells us there can be hope for the future.

First, there is hope of a changed person. No matter how hard we try, we are incapable of ridding ourselves of the selfishness and greed that cause conflict and strife and war. Our only hope is a changed heart—and Jesus is in the business of changing hearts.

Second, there is hope of a changed world. When we know Christ, He gives us by His Spirit a new love and concern for others. We can no longer be indifferent to their sufferings, and we'll want to do something about them. Changed by Christ, we can begin to change our world.

Third, there is hope of an unchanging eternity in heaven. This world is not all there is. Someday all its pain and heartache will come to an end for those who know Christ (Revelation 21:4). Evil and death will be abolished, and we will be safely in God's presence forever.

As you read the headlines or look at your own life, you may be wondering if there is any hope. The answer from the Bible is a resounding yes.

—BILLY GRAHAM

GOD'S WORDS FOR YOU, GRANDPA

"My Father's will is that everyone who looks to the Son and believes in him shall have eternal life, and I will raise them up at the last day."

JOHN 6:40

"I give them eternal life, and they shall never perish; no one will snatch them out of my hand."

JOHN 10:28

Consider the blameless, observe the upright; a future awaits those who seek peace.

PSALM 37:37

"I say to all of you: From now on you will see the Son of Man sitting at the right hand of the Mighty One and coming on the clouds of heaven."

MATTHEW 26:64

"Consecrate yourselves, for tomorrow the LORD will do amazing things among you."

JOSHUA 3:5

I am convinced that neither death nor life, neither angels nor demons, neither the present nor the future, nor any powers, neither height nor depth, nor anything else in all creation, will be able to separate us from the love of God that is in Christ Jesus our Lord.

ROMANS 8:38-39

"In the beginning, Lord, you laid the foundations of the earth, and the heavens are the work of your hands. They will perish, but you remain; they will all wear out like a garment. You will roll them up like a robe; like a garment they will be changed. But you remain the same, and your years will never end."

HEBREWS 1:10-12

Know also that wisdom is like honey for you: If you find it, there is a future hope for you, and your hope will not be cut off.

PROVERBS 24:14

"The Lord will guide you always; he will satisfy your needs in a sun-scorched land and will strengthen your frame. You will be like a well-watered garden, like a spring whose waters never fail."

ISAIAH 58:11

"Give, and it will be given to you. A **GOOD** measure, pressed down, shaken together and running over, will be poured into your lap. For with the **MEASURE** you use, it will be measured to you."

LUKE 6:38

19

GENUINE FAITH

A true disciple of Jesus is a giver. Not just any kind of a giver, but a generous giver! The motivation for the believer should always be the example demonstrated by our Savior, Jesus Christ. Just as Jesus gave of Himself to meet our spiritual needs, we should always be quick to give generously to meet the needs of others.

When the apostle Paul wrote to the Corinthians, the Jerusalem church was experiencing deep poverty. The Corinthian believers had promised to give to help alleviate some of the Jerusalem believers' pain. Paul admonished them to be generous. He wanted their generosity to prove their faith.

The Corinthians gave joyfully to assist those in need, and their giving brought tremendous results. Jewish believers who had been skeptical of the Gentiles' faith saw by their actions that their faith was genuine. These Jewish believers also knew heartfelt gratitude to God for those who, in the spirit of Christ, had helped meet their needs. God was glorified.

As the Corinthians obeyed God by generously giving, they proclaimed the life-changing power of the gospel.

How good a giver are you?

—From *God Is Faithful*

"Bring the whole tithe into the storehouse, that there may be food in my house. Test me in this," says the LORD Almighty, "and see if I will not throw open the floodgates of heaven and pour out so much blessing that there will not be room enough to store it."

MALACHI 3:10

"Store up for yourselves treasures in heaven, where moths and vermin do not destroy, and where thieves do not break in and steal. For where your treasure is, there your heart will be also."

MATTHEW 6:20–21

"It is more blessed to give than to receive."

ACTS 20:35

God is not unjust; he will not forget your work and the love you have shown him as you have helped his people and continue to help them.

HEBREWS 6:10

Do not forget to do good and to share with others, for with such sacrifices God is pleased.

HEBREWS 13:16

"Freely you have received; freely give."

MATTHEW 10:8

"Give to the one who asks you, and do not turn away from the one who wants to borrow from you."

MATTHEW 5:42

Make every effort to add to your faith . . . mutual affection; and to mutual affection, love.

2 PETER 1:5, 7

"In your unfailing love you will lead the people you have redeemed."

EXODUS 15:13

He will cover you with his **FEATHERS**,

and under his **WINGS** you will find refuge;

his faithfulness will be your

SHIELD and rampart.

PSALM 91:4

20
THE BEST THING TO COME

Because he delights in me, he saved me" (Psalm 18:19 NCV).

And you thought He saved you because of your decency. You thought He saved you because of your good works or good attitude or good looks. Sorry. If that were the case, your salvation would be lost when your voice went south or your works got weak. There are many reasons God saves you: to bring glory to Himself, to appease His justice, to demonstrate His sovereignty. But one of the sweetest reasons God saved you is because He is fond of you. He likes having you around. He thinks you are the best thing to come down the pike in quite a while. "As a man rejoices over his new wife, so your God will rejoice over you" (Isaiah 62:5 NCV).

If God had a refrigerator, your picture would be on it. If He had a wallet, your photo would be in it. He sends you flowers every spring and a sunrise every morning. Whenever you want to talk, He'll listen. He can live anywhere in the universe, and He chose your heart. And the Christmas gift He sent you in Bethlehem? Face it, friend. He's crazy about you.

—MAX LUCADO

GOD'S WORDS FOR YOU, GRANDPA

God is faithful, who has called you into fellowship with his Son, Jesus Christ our Lord.

1 CORINTHIANS 1:9

He is the Rock, his works are perfect, and all his ways are just. A faithful God who does no wrong, upright and just is he.

DEUTERONOMY 32:4

LORD, you are my God; I will exalt you and praise your name, for in perfect faithfulness you have done wonderful things, things planned long ago.

ISAIAH 25:1

The LORD is good and his love endures forever; his faithfulness continues through all generations.

PSALM 100:5

Let us hold unswervingly to the hope we profess, for he who promised is faithful.

HEBREWS 10:23

Praise be to the LORD, for he showed me the wonders of his love.
PSALM 31:21

He is the faithful God, keeping his covenant of love to a thousand generations of those who love him and keep his commandments.
DEUTERONOMY 7:9

"God is not human, that he should lie, not a human being, that he should change his mind. Does he speak and then not act? Does he promise and not fulfill?"
NUMBERS 23:19

The Lord is faithful, and he will strengthen you and protect you from the evil one.
2 THESSALONIANS 3:3

"To the faithful you show yourself faithful, to the blameless you show yourself blameless."
2 SAMUEL 22:26

"In all that has happened to us, you have remained righteous; you have acted faithfully."
NEHEMIAH 9:33

We love because he first loved us.
1 JOHN 4:19

To those who have been called, who are **LOVED** in God the Father and kept for Jesus Christ: Mercy, **PEACE** and love be yours in abundance.

JUDE VV. 1–2

21

BOUNTIFUL HARVEST

I t is often into broken ground that the seeds of spring are planted; they germinate to grow into a bountiful harvest. And it is into broken hearts that God, in love, plants His Word to save and prepare His people for some great work. . . . Who can describe or measure the love of God? When we read of God's justice, it is justice tempered with love. When we read of God's righteousness, it is righteousness founded on love. When we read of God's atonement for sin, it is atonement necessitated because of His love, provided by His love, finished by His love.

When we read about the resurrection of Christ, we see the miracle of His love. When we read about the abiding presence of Christ, we know the power of His love. When we read about the return of Christ, we long for the fulfillment of His love.

No matter how black, dirty, shameful, or terrible our sin, God will forgive. We may be at the very gate of hell itself, but He will be reaching out in everlasting love.

—BILLY GRAHAM

GOD'S WORDS FOR YOU, GRANDPA

I am convinced that neither death nor life, neither angels nor demons, neither the present nor the future, nor any powers, neither height nor depth, nor anything else in all creation, will be able to separate us from the love of God that is in Christ Jesus our Lord.

ROMANS 8:38–39

Your love, LORD, reaches to the heavens, your faithfulness to the skies.

PSALM 36:5

According to your love remember me, for you, LORD, are good.

PSALM 25:7

See what great love the Father has lavished on us, that we should be called children of God! And that is what we are!

1 JOHN 3:1

How priceless is your unfailing love, O God! People take refuge in the shadow of your wings.

PSALM 36:7

I will sing of the LORD's great love forever; with my mouth I will make your faithfulness known through all generations.

I pray that you, being rooted and established in love, may have power, together with all the Lord's holy people, to grasp how wide and long and high and deep is the love of Christ.

EPHESIANS 3:17–18

For God so loved the world that he gave his one and only Son, that whoever believes in him shall not perish but have eternal life.

JOHN 3:16

This is love: not that we loved God, but that he loved us and sent his Son as an atoning sacrifice for our sins.

1 JOHN 4:10

You, Lord, are forgiving and good, abounding in love to all who call to you.

PSALM 86:5

From **EVERLASTING** to everlasting

the LORD's love is with those

who fear him,

and his **RIGHTEOUSNESS**

with their children's children—

with those who keep his **COVENANT**

and remember to obey his precepts.

PSALM 103:17–18

88

22

WHOLLY PERFECT

I am looking at a picture received yesterday of my latest grandchild—a picture taken the very day of his birth. I have many happy and grateful thoughts as I gaze at it, but beneath them all is a wonderment amounting to awe.

Here he is, this little man, every feature and organ intact and in place, the intricately balanced whole perfectly adapted to his intricately complicated new environment. In the wildest flight of fancy can we conceive of a miracle more miraculous than this? And yet no less amazing and inexplicable, no less wonderful, is every common thing in our common life; and we should be able to see it so if we were able to keep this baby's fresh, new eyes.

God reveals to babes what is hidden from the wise and prudent and that only to the extent we are able to turn, and become like little children, is it given us to see the kingdom of God.

—JOHN KNOX

GOD'S WORDS FOR YOU, GRANDPA

May the LORD bless you from Zion; may you see the prosperity of Jerusalem all the days of your life. May you live to see your children's children.

PSALM 128:5-6

Children's children are a crown to the aged, and parents are the pride of their children.

PROVERBS 17:6

Children are a heritage from the LORD.

PSALM 127:3

The Spirit you received does not make you slaves, so that you live in fear again; rather, the Spirit you received brought about your adoption to sonship.

ROMANS 8:15

In Christ Jesus you are all children of God through faith.

GALATIANS 3:26

"Come now, let us settle the matter," says the LORD. "Though your sins are like scarlet, they shall be as white as snow; though they are red as crimson, they shall be like wool."

ISAIAH 1:18

"I, even I, am he who blots out your transgressions, for my own sake, and remembers your sins no more."

ISAIAH 43:25

Praise the LORD, my soul, and forget not all his benefits—who forgives all your sins and heals all your diseases.

PSALM 103:2-3

EVEN when I am old and gray,

do not forsake me, my God,

till I declare your **POWER**

to the next generation,

your mighty acts to all who are to come.

PSALM 71:18

23

NO DUPLICATION

L aps open and ready for watching post-nap cartoons. Eyes crinkling in response to cartwheels and somersaults across the backyard. Heads thrown back in laughter during tickle sessions. Checks hidden in birthday cards. Games played on tables still sticky from holiday baking. Walks, hand in hand, through the leaves in the park. Ice cream on cones, stacked scoop upon scoop, licked in unison on an outside bench. Wrinkly hands curled atop piano keys while others gather around to listen.

Grandparents—we all bring offerings that no other can duplicate: An offering of wisdom that comes from living a lifetime. An offering of patience hewn from trial. An offering of laughter learned through making the most of both prosperous and lean times. Indeed, we "still bear fruit in old age." We "stay fresh and green" no matter our age (Psalm 92:14)! Let's thank God for the gift of being a grandparent.

—ELISA MORGAN

GOD'S WORDS FOR YOU, GRANDPA

The righteous will flourish like a palm tree, they will grow like a cedar of Lebanon; planted in the house of the LORD, they will flourish in the courts of our God. They will still bear fruit in old age, they will stay fresh and green.

PSALM 92:12–14

Whoever fears the LORD has a secure fortress, and for their children it will be a refuge.

PROVERBS 14:26

"I will make a covenant of peace with them and rid the land of savage beasts so that they may live in the wilderness and sleep in the forests in safety. I will make them and the places surrounding my hill a blessing. I will send down showers in season; there will be showers of blessing. The trees will yield their fruit and the ground will yield its crops; the people will be secure in their land. They will know that I am the LORD."

EZEKIEL 34:25–27

The God of peace will be with you.

PHILIPPIANS 4:9

I will open my mouth with a parable; I will utter hidden things, things from of old—things we have heard and known, things our ancestors have told us. We will not hide them from their descendants; we will tell the next generation the praiseworthy deeds of the LORD, his power, and the wonders he has done.

PSALM 78:2-4

Grace and peace to you from him who is, and who was, and who is to come.

REVELATION 1:4

Love and faithfulness meet together; righteousness and peace kiss each other.

PSALM 85:10

If it is possible, as far as it depends on you, live at peace with everyone.

ROMANS 12:18

Peacemakers who sow in peace reap a harvest of righteousness.

JAMES 3:18

Give **PRAISE** to the LORD,

proclaim his name;

make known among the **NATIONS**

what he has done.

1 CHRONICLES 16:8

24

GIVING GOOD GIFTS

God is the source of every good gift. God has given us everything good to enjoy, including rain to make things grow, minerals to make the soil fertile, animals for food and clothing, and energy for industry and transportation. Everything we have is from Him.

Jesus said, "If you, then, though you are evil, know how to give good gifts to your children, how much more will your Father in heaven give good gifts to those who ask him!" (Matthew 7:11). Paul added, "For everything God created is good, and nothing is to be rejected if it is received with thanksgiving, because it is consecrated by the word of God and prayer" (1 Timothy 4:4–5).

Sadly, unbelievers don't acknowledge God's goodness, though they benefit from it every day. They attribute His providential care to luck or fate. They do not honor Him as God or give Him thanks (Romans 1:21).

How sad to see such ingratitude, yet how thrilling to know that the infinite God cares for us and supplies our every need. Don't ever take His provisions for granted! Look to Him daily and receive His gifts with a thankful heart.

—JOHN F. MACARTHUR JR.

GOD'S WORDS FOR YOU, GRANDPA

Give thanks in all circumstances; for this is God's will for you in Christ Jesus.

1 THESSALONIANS 5:18

Thanks be to God! He gives us the victory through our Lord Jesus Christ.

1 CORINTHIANS 15:57

I will give thanks to the LORD because of his righteousness; I will sing the praises of the name of the LORD Most High.

PSALM 7:17

Give thanks to the LORD, for he is good; his love endures forever. Let the redeemed of the LORD tell their story.

PSALM 107:1–2

Just as you received Christ Jesus as Lord, continue to live your lives in him, rooted and built up in him, strengthened in the faith as you were taught, and overflowing with thankfulness.

COLOSSIANS 2:6–7

Thanks be to God, who always leads us as captives in Christ's triumphal procession and uses us to spread the aroma of the knowledge of him everywhere.

2 CORINTHIANS 2:14

Let them give thanks to the LORD for his unfailing love and his wonderful deeds for mankind.

PSALM 107:21

You turned my wailing into dancing; you removed my sackcloth and clothed me with joy, that my heart may sing your praises and not be silent. LORD my God, I will praise you forever.

PSALM 30:11–12

Come, let us sing for joy to the LORD; let us shout aloud to the Rock of our salvation. Let us come before him with thanksgiving and extol him with music and song.

PSALM 95:1–2

Praise the LORD. I will extol the LORD with all my heart in the council of the upright and in the assembly. Great are the works of the LORD; they are pondered by all who delight in them.

PSALM 111:1–2

He spreads out the northern

SKIES over empty space;

he suspends the earth over nothing. . . .

By his **BREATH** the skies became fair;

his hand pierced the gliding serpent.

And these are but the outer fringe of his works;

how faint the whisper we hear of him!

Who then can understand the

THUNDER of his power?

JOB 26:7, 13–14

25

UNUSED POWER

How fast will your car go? Maybe 130 . . . 140 . . . 150 miles per hour? And you've probably never even approached 100, right? Wow, just think of all that raw, unused power!

If you're mechanically inclined, you know actually driving at those speeds often could seriously damage your engine.

In your job as a grandfather, you have a high-powered disciplinary engine with its own imaginary speedometer. This instrument registers numbers much higher than safe speed limits. Do you have the right to push your accelerator to the floor? Of course you do. But most experts agree that if you spend too much time at those high speeds, you'll do harm.

Sometimes grandfathers are called upon to use their power. Yet it's usually better to hold back, leaving some of that force unused.

God's restraint—His mercy and His grace—is what makes Him so awesome. His tenderness and patience melt our defiance and realign our wayward hearts.

Perhaps you need to discover the power of unused power. Your family will be grateful.

—Robert Wolgemuth

GOD'S WORDS FOR YOU, GRANDPA

"With God all things are possible."
MATTHEW 19:26

"I am the LORD, the God of all mankind. Is anything too hard for me?"
JEREMIAH 32:27

The LORD is slow to anger but great in power; the LORD will not leave the guilty unpunished. His way is in the whirlwind and the storm, and clouds are the dust of his feet.
NAHUM 1:3

[We pray] that you may live a life worthy of the Lord and please him in every way: bearing fruit in every good work, growing in the knowledge of God, being strengthened with all power according to his glorious might so that you may have great endurance and patience.
COLOSSIANS 1:10-11

"Your strength will equal your days."
DEUTERONOMY 33:25

"I will strengthen them in the LORD and in his name they will live securely," declares the LORD.

ZECHARIAH 10:12

Be strong in the Lord and in his mighty power.

EPHESIANS 6:10

He has made everything beautiful in its time. He has also set eternity in the human heart; yet no one can fathom what God has done from beginning to end.

ECCLESIASTES 3:11

"You will receive power when the Holy Spirit comes on you; and you will be my witnesses in Jerusalem, and in all Judea and Samaria, and to the ends of the earth."

ACTS 1:8

You may say to yourself, "My power and the strength of my hands have produced this wealth for me." But remember the LORD your God, for it is he who gives you the ability to produce wealth, and so confirms his covenant.

DEUTERONOMY 8:17–18

As for me, I am filled with power, with the Spirit of the LORD, and with justice and might.

MICAH 3:8

PRAISE the LORD, my soul,

and forget not all his benefits—

who forgives all your sins

and **HEALS** all your diseases,

who redeems your life from the pit

and **CROWNS** you with

love and compassion.

PSALM 103:2-4

26

ULTIMATE HEALING

If you are sick, cry out to Jesus!

He will heal you—instantly or gradually or ultimately.

He may heal you instantly. One word was enough for Him to banish demons, heal epilepsy, and raise the dead. He may do this for you.

Or He may heal you gradually. In the case of a blind man from Bethsaida, Jesus healed him in stages (Mark 8:22–26).

And don't forget the story of Lazarus. By the time Jesus reached the cemetery, Lazarus had been in the tomb four days. But Jesus called him out. Did Jesus heal Lazarus? Yes, dramatically, but not immediately (John 11:1–44).

Our highest hope, however, is in our ultimate healing. In heaven God will restore our bodies to their intended splendor. "We know that when He is revealed, we shall be like Him" (1 John 3:2 NKJV). God will turn your tomb into a womb out of which you will be born with a perfect body into a perfect world. In the meantime keep praying. *Father, You are good. I need help. Heal me.*

—MAX LUCADO

Surely he took up our pain and bore our suffering, yet we considered him punished by God, stricken by him, and afflicted. But he was pierced for our transgressions, he was crushed for our iniquities; the punishment that brought us peace was on him, and by his wounds we are healed.

ISAIAH 53:4–5

Jesus went throughout Galilee, teaching in their synagogues, proclaiming the good news of the kingdom, and healing every disease and sickness among the people.

MATTHEW 4:23

You restored me to health and let me live.

ISAIAH 38:16

Is anyone among you sick? Let them call the elders of the church to pray over them and anoint them with oil in the name of the Lord. And the prayer offered in faith will make the sick person well; the Lord will raise them up.

JAMES 5:14–15

I pray that you may enjoy good health and that all may go well with you, even as your soul is getting along well.

3 JOHN V. 2

"I will heal my people and will let them enjoy abundant peace and security."

JEREMIAH 33:6

Heal me, LORD, and I will be healed; save me and I will be saved, for you are the one I praise.

JEREMIAH 17:14

Pay attention to what I say; turn your ear to my words. Do not let them out of your sight, keep them within your heart; for they are life to those who find them and health to one's whole body.

PROVERBS 4:20-22

"He himself bore our sins" in his body on the cross, so that we might die to sins and live for righteousness; "by his wounds you have been healed."

1 PETER 2:24

"My Father's **HOUSE** has many rooms; if that were not so, would I have told you that I am going there to prepare a place for you? And if I go and prepare a **PLACE** for you, I will come back and take you to be with me that you also may be where I am."

JOHN 14:2-3

27

DOOR TO ETERNITY

John, the old visionary, was allowed to have a brief view through the door to eternity. In the last book of the Bible, he presented what he saw but not in a logical discourse. He painted a picture for us. He showed us through his eyes.

He saw many things, but one thing stood out: the throne of God. That throne drew all of John's attention. The splendor was so overwhelming, and the glitter of something like a glass sea around the throne so blinding, that John actually could not see God. He saw only the shining reflection, which reminded him of diamonds. Even John's sanctified, inspired eye could not see God in a vision. So great is God's glory that no eye has ever seen Him.

That is the heart of what heaven will be like: We shall see God. We can only be still in amazement: to see God and not to be last, to see God and live. We shall never be weary of looking at Him, for we shall never see everything. We shall fall from one ecstasy into the next.

To enter heaven and to see Jesus; to enjoy the company of the Redeemer. When I think of that, a strong desire to be there gets hold of me.

—CORNELIS GILHUIS

GOD'S WORDS FOR YOU, GRANDPA

God raised us up with Christ and seated us with him in the
heavenly realms in Christ Jesus.

EPHESIANS 2:6

"See, I will create new heavens and a new earth. The former
things will not be remembered, nor will they come to mind."

ISAIAH 65:17

In keeping with his promise we are looking forward to a new
heaven and a new earth, where righteousness dwells.

2 PETER 3:13

The Lord himself will come down from heaven, with a loud
command, with the voice of the archangel and with the trumpet
call of God, and the dead in Christ will rise first. After that, we
who are still alive and are left will be caught up together with
them in the clouds to meet the Lord in the air. And so we will be
with the Lord forever.

1 THESSALONIANS 4:16–17

"Look, I am coming soon! My reward is with me, and I will give to each person according to what they have done."

REVELATION 22:12

The angel showed me the river of the water of life, as clear as crystal, flowing from the throne of God and of the Lamb down the middle of the great street of the city.

REVELATION 22:1–2

The city does not need the sun or the moon to shine on it, for the glory of God gives it light, and the Lamb is its lamp. The nations will walk by its light, and the kings of the earth will bring their splendor into it. On no day will its gates ever be shut, for there will be no night there. The glory and honor of the nations will be brought into it. Nothing impure will ever enter it, nor will anyone who does what is shameful or deceitful, but only those whose names are written in the Lamb's book of life.

REVELATION 21:23–27

The angel said to me, "Write this: Blessed are those who are invited to the wedding supper of the Lamb!" And he added, "These are the true words of God."

REVELATION 19:9

We say with confidence,

"The LORD is my **HELPER**;

I will not be afraid.

What can mere

MORTALS do to me?"

HEBREWS 13:6

28
NEVER TOO LATE

When we were younger, most of us earnestly sought to discover God's plan for our lives. Are we equally diligent in seeking His plan for our old age, or are we just drifting along with no definite aim or goal?

With more time to review the past, we may become discouraged as we recall opportunities missed, a lessening of zeal in God's service, a mediocre prayer life, or perhaps actual sins of which we have reason to be ashamed. It is at such moments of introspection that we need to turn our eyes outward and upward to our loving and understanding Father. Romans 5:20 says, "Where sin increased, grace increased all the more."

The wonderful thing about God's abundant grace and favor is that it is never too late to discover and follow God's plan for the remainder of our lives, never too late to make a new start.

To disillusioned compatriots, the prophet Joel brought an inspiring message of hope—the hope of a new beginning: "I will repay you for the years the locusts have eaten" (2:25).

—J. Oswald Sanders

GOD'S WORDS FOR YOU, GRANDPA

We have put our hope in the living God, who is the Savior of all people, and especially of those who believe.

1 TIMOTHY 4:10

Put your hope in the LORD both now and forevermore.

PSALM 131:3

Guide me in your truth and teach me, for you are God my Savior, and my hope is in you all day long.

PSALM 25:5

Hope does not put us to shame, because God's love has been poured out into our hearts through the Holy Spirit, who has been given to us.

ROMANS 5:5

Why, my soul, are you downcast? Why so disturbed within me? Put your hope in God, for I will yet praise him, my Savior and my God.

PSALM 42:11

Your hands made me and formed me; give me understanding to learn your commands. May those who fear you rejoice when they see me, for I have put my hope in your word.

PSALM 119:73-74

Yet this I call to mind and therefore I have hope: Because of the LORD's great love we are not consumed, for his compassions never fail. . . . The LORD is good to those whose hope is in him, to the one who seeks him.

LAMENTATIONS 3:21-22, 25

The eyes of the LORD are on those who fear him, on those whose hope is in his unfailing love. . . . May your unfailing love be with us, LORD, even as we put our hope in you.

PSALM 33:18, 22

Put your hope in the LORD, for with the LORD is unfailing love and with him is full redemption.

PSALM 130:7

May our Lord Jesus Christ himself and God our Father, who loved us and by his grace gave us eternal encouragement and good hope, encourage your hearts and strengthen you in every good deed and word.

2 THESSALONIANS 2:16-17

The Lord will rescue me from every evil

attack and will bring me **SAFELY**

to his heavenly kingdom. To him

be **GLORY** for ever and ever.

2 TIMOTHY 4:18

29
LOOK AHEAD

We who love the Lord are to hate sin. Indeed, the Christian life is a battle against it. That's why we are equipped to be soldiers (Ephesians 6). Sometimes the veterans get tired and decide to leave warfare to the young recruits. Fighting for truth and justice is wearying.

Moses was past eighty when he led the Israelites out of Egypt. The next forty years were full of fighting. Moses got weary. At 120 Moses was still warning the people about sin.

In Hebrews 11 it says, "He regarded disgrace for the sake of Christ as of greater value than the treasures of Egypt, because he was looking ahead to his reward" (v. 26). Looking ahead. Anticipating the day when he would be with the Lord.

When we feel like quitting—retiring or even going AWOL—let us remember Moses and look ahead. When we have fought the last battle, God stands ready to welcome us to eternal peace.

—JEAN SHAW

GOD'S WORDS FOR YOU, GRANDPA

If anybody does sin, we have an advocate with the Father—Jesus Christ, the Righteous One.

1 JOHN 2:1

All have sinned and fall short of the glory of God, and all are justified freely by his grace through the redemption that came by Christ Jesus.

ROMANS 3:23–24

Through Christ Jesus the law of the Spirit who gives life has set you free from the law of sin and death.

ROMANS 8:2

We all, like sheep, have gone astray, each of us has turned to our own way; and the LORD has laid on him the iniquity of us all.

ISAIAH 53:6

Our struggle is not against flesh and blood, but against the . . . authorities, against the powers of this dark world and against the spiritual forces of evil in the heavenly realms.

EPHESIANS 6:12

No temptation has overtaken you except what is common to mankind. And God is faithful; he will not let you be tempted beyond what you can bear. But when you are tempted, he will also provide a way out so that you can endure it.

1 CORINTHIANS 10:13

I acknowledged my sin to you and did not cover up my iniquity. I said, "I will confess my transgressions to the LORD." And you forgave the guilt of my sin.

PSALM 32:5

Count yourselves dead to sin but alive to God in Christ Jesus.

ROMANS 6:11

"The joy of the LORD is your strength."

NEHEMIAH 8:10

The LORD has done great things for us, and we are filled with joy.

PSALM 126:3

The precepts of the LORD are right, giving joy to the heart. The commands of the LORD are radiant, giving light to the eyes.

PSALM 19:8

Your statutes are my heritage forever; they are the joy of my heart.

PSALM 119:111

I delight greatly in the LORD;

my **SOUL** rejoices in my God.

For he has clothed me with

garments of **SALVATION**

and arrayed me in a robe of his righteousness,

as a bridegroom **ADORNS**

his head like a priest,

and as a bride adorns herself with her jewels.

ISAIAH 61:10

30

INVISIBLE REALITIES

We are deluged by the visible—a world in chaos, a nation divided, financial struggles, family problems, physical ailments. When our focus is limited to the visible, we grow frightened. But when we realize invisible realities are at play, we cannot lose heart. With spiritual eyes we see the Father, the Son, and the Holy Spirit. We see God's holy angels surrounding the earth. We trust in the qualities of God. We believe God's promises and wait with earnest expectation for their unstoppable fulfillment. And we yearn for heaven. These unseen realities are greater than the negative realities surrounding us.

When you awaken each morning, envision God standing there to greet you. As you drive to work, speak to Him naturally, as if He were in the passenger seat. Before an appointment, whisper a prayer for His help. As you relax at the end of the day, your work behind you, remember the angels hovering near. As you turn down the covers of your bed, remember you are blanketed with the promises of God. As you fall asleep, ponder your heavenly home.

God is closer than you know, and His unseen grace will, in His timing, overturn all of life's unseemly moments.

—ROBERT J. MORGAN

GOD'S WORDS FOR YOU, GRANDPA

Light shines on the righteous and joy on the upright in heart.

PSALM 97:11

His favor lasts a lifetime; weeping may stay for the night, but rejoicing comes in the morning.

PSALM 30:5

May all who seek you rejoice and be glad in you; may those who long for your saving help always say, "The LORD is great!"

PSALM 70:4

Let all who take refuge in you be glad; let them ever sing for joy. Spread your protection over them, that those who love your name may rejoice in you.

PSALM 5:11

The prospect of the righteous is joy.

PROVERBS 10:28

Be glad, people of Zion, rejoice in the LORD your God, for he has given you the autumn rains because he is faithful. He sends you abundant showers, both autumn and spring rains, as before.

JOEL 2:23

"Until now you have not asked for anything in my name. Ask and you will receive, and your joy will be complete."

JOHN 16:24

Those the LORD has rescued will return. They will enter Zion with singing; everlasting joy will crown their heads. Gladness and joy will overtake them, and sorrow and sighing will flee away.

ISAIAH 51:11

The LORD your God will bless you in all your harvest and in all the work of your hands, and your joy will be complete.

DEUTERONOMY 16:15

You make known to me the path of life; you will fill me with joy in your presence, with eternal pleasures at your right hand.

PSALM 16:11

Nebuchadnezzar said, "Praise be to the God of Shadrach, Meshach and Abednego, who has sent his **ANGEL** and rescued his servants! They **TRUSTED** in him and defied the king's command and were willing to give up their lives rather than serve or **WORSHIP** any god except their own God."

DANIEL 3:28

31
STRONGER THAN DEATH

The resurrection is the expression of God's faithfulness to Jesus and to all God's children. Through the resurrection God has said to Jesus, "You are indeed My beloved Son, and My love is everlasting," and to us God has said, "You indeed are My beloved children, and My love is everlasting." The resurrection is God's way of revealing to us that nothing that belongs to God will ever go to waste. What belongs to God will never get lost.

The resurrection doesn't answer any of our curious questions about life after death, such as, How will it be? How will it look? But it does reveal to us that, indeed, love is stronger than death. After that revelation, we must remain silent, leave the whys, wheres, hows, and whens behind, and simply trust.

As the father of the epileptic boy, who asked Jesus to heal his child, we will always have to say, "I do believe; help me overcome my unbelief!" (Mark 9:24). Still, when we keep our eyes fixed on the risen Lord, we may find not only that love is stronger than death but also that our faith is stronger than our skepticism.

—Henri J. M. Nouwen

"Do not let your hearts be troubled. You believe in God; believe also in me."

JOHN 14:1

He has delivered us from such a deadly peril, and he will deliver us again. On him we have set our hope that he will continue to deliver us.

2 CORINTHIANS 1:10

Those who know your name trust in you, for you, LORD, have never forsaken those who seek you.

PSALM 9:10

Trust in the LORD forever, for the LORD, the LORD himself, is the Rock eternal.

ISAIAH 26:4

Those who trust in the LORD are like Mount Zion, which cannot be shaken but endures forever.

PSALM 125:1

It is better to take refuge in the Lord than to trust in humans. It is better to take refuge in the Lord than to trust in princes.

PSALM 118:8-9

Why, my soul, are you downcast? Why so disturbed within me? Put your hope in God, for I will yet praise him, my Savior and my God.

PSALM 42:5

Whoever gives heed to instruction prospers, and blessed is the one who trusts in the Lord.

PROVERBS 16:20

Those who trust in the Lord will prosper.

PROVERBS 28:25

"Anyone who believes in him will never be put to shame."

ROMANS 10:11

Fear of man will prove to be a snare, but whoever trusts in the Lord is kept safe.

PROVERBS 29:25

"Be **STRONG** and very courageous.
Be careful to obey all the law my servant
Moses gave you . . . that you may be
SUCCESSFUL wherever you
go. Keep this Book of the Law always
on your lips; meditate on it day and
night, so that you may be careful to do
everything written in it. Then you will be
PROSPEROUS and successful."

JOSHUA 1:7–8

32

HAPPY FAMILY

L et's take a little journey back to geometry class. We're going to discuss postulates. For an example, let's try a family postulate. If I am a father and my child gives birth to a baby, then I am a grandfather. If I make a rule and my grandchild disobeys me, then I have some disciplining work to do. Since the first part of each statement is true, and since the second part of each statement is also true, then the combination of the first and second parts makes each conclusion true for sure. See how these work?

In Deuteronomy 30 we have an amazing postulate. It starts with verse 1 and ends with verse 3. Moses presented this amazing postulate to the Israelites in terms they could clearly understand: Since God can be taken at His word, if He finds you obedient to His law, then He will "restore your fortunes and have compassion on you" (v. 3).

While theologians will arm-wrestle over the kind of "prosperity" God is referring to here, it's indisputable that He does promise the kind of success that is consistent within His economy—where a foreign import can be bought with lunch money and where a happy family is a priceless treasure.

—ROBERT WOLGEMUTH

GOD'S WORDS FOR YOU, GRANDPA

[King Uzziah] sought God during the days of Zechariah, who instructed him in the fear of God. As long as he sought the LORD, God gave him success.

2 CHRONICLES 26:5

May he give you the desire of your heart and make all your plans succeed. May we shout for joy over your victory and lift up our banners in the name of our God. May the LORD grant all your requests.

PSALM 20:4–5

Blessed is the one who does not walk in step with the wicked or stand in the way that sinners take or sit in the company of mockers, but whose delight is in the law of the LORD, and who meditates on his law day and night. That person is like a tree planted by streams of water, which yields its fruit in season and whose leaf does not wither—whatever they do prospers.

PSALM 1:1–3

Plans fail for lack of counsel, but with many advisers they succeed.

PROVERBS 15:22

Hezekiah trusted in the LORD, the God of Israel. There was no one like him among all the kings of Judah, either before him or after him. He held fast to the LORD and did not stop following him; he kept the commands the LORD had given Moses. And the LORD was with him; he was successful in whatever he undertook.

2 KINGS 18:5-7

"Have faith in the LORD your God and you will be upheld; have faith in his prophets and you will be successful."

2 CHRONICLES 20:20

When his master saw that the LORD was with him and that the LORD gave him success in everything he did, Joseph found favor in his eyes and became his attendant. Potiphar put him in charge of his household, and he entrusted to his care everything he owned.

GENESIS 39:3-4

In everything that [King Hezekiah] undertook in the service of God's temple . . . he sought his God and worked wholeheartedly. And so he prospered.

2 CHRONICLES 31:21

Commit to the LORD whatever you do, and he will establish your plans.

PROVERBS 16:3

Be **KIND** and compassionate to one
another, **FORGIVING** each other,

just as in Christ God forgave you.

EPHESIANS 4:32

132

33

ECHOES OF WISDOM

J umping in with good advice is our natural reaction to any problem our grandchildren have. But resisting the urge to shower them with the benefit of our great wisdom is the sign of a good listener.

By taking the time to listen for feelings and echo back what we hear, we enable our grandchildren to see and understand more clearly what is going on in their lives. This helps them learn to take the steps necessary toward solving their own problems. By asking questions, you show them you are really attentive to what they are saying. Because this is a compliment to your grandchildren, their response is likely to come more readily.

Some of us are especially tempted to overwhelm our grandchildren with spiritual and scriptural answers, many of which can come across as frustratingly pat. Instead of listening to what the kids are saying, we spend our time watching for an opening where we can present our own point of view. There's nothing wrong with sharing your wisdom. It's an important part of teaching—if you wait for your grandchildren to ask for it and if you have listened enough to earn the right to share it.

—JAN STOOP AND BETTY SOUTHARD

GOD'S WORDS FOR YOU, GRANDPA

The Holy Spirit says: "Today, if you hear his voice, do not harden your hearts as you did in the rebellion, during the time of testing in the wilderness."

HEBREWS 3:7-8

Whoever heeds life-giving correction will be at home among the wise.

PROVERBS 15:31

"Everyone who has heard the Father and learned from him comes to me."

JOHN 6:45

"Here I am! I stand at the door and knock. If anyone hears my voice and opens the door, I will come in and eat with that person, and they with me."

REVELATION 3:20

I am convinced that neither death nor life, neither angels nor demons, neither the present nor the future, nor any powers, neither height nor depth, nor anything else in all creation, will be able to separate us from the love of God that is in Christ Jesus our Lord.

ROMANS 8:38–39

Come near to God and he will come near to you.

JAMES 4:8

Praise be to God, who has not rejected my prayer or withheld his love from me!

PSALM 66:20

I call to God, and the LORD saves me.

PSALM 55:16

God has said, "Never will I leave you; never will I forsake you."

HEBREWS 13:5

"Though the **MOUNTAINS** be shaken

and the hills be removed,

yet my **UNFAILING** love for you

will not be shaken

nor my covenant of peace be removed,"

says the LORD, who has

COMPASSION on you.

ISAIAH 54:10

34
GREATEST SOURCE

Many people remain lonely because they fear rejection. They think rejection hurts worse than loneliness and spend much of their time and money trying to avoid it. But that is a wrong attitude. Those who expect to be rejected usually will feel that they are. Those who expect to receive friendship and comfort usually will.

When you need friendship and comfort, offer friendship and comfort, and don't expect rejection. Accept yourself where you are, whatever your need, and remember that Christ will not reject you. When you reach out to Him, He will always respond with loving acceptance. He said in Matthew 7:11, "If you then, being evil, know how to give good things to your children [and your friends and all those around you], how much more will your Father who is in heaven give good things to those who ask Him!" (NKJV).

Your greatest source of comfort and hope is Christ Jesus.
—DR. DAVID JEREMIAH

GOD'S WORDS FOR YOU, GRANDPA

In Christ we, though many, form one body, and each member belongs to all the others.

ROMANS 12:5

"Be strong and courageous. Do not be afraid or terrified because of them, for the LORD your God goes with you; he will never leave you nor forsake you."

DEUTERONOMY 31:6

I am always with you; you hold me by my right hand.

PSALM 73:23

"Surely I am with you always, to the very end of the age."

MATTHEW 28:20

"I will not leave you as orphans; I will come to you."

JOHN 14:18

He heals the brokenhearted and binds up their wounds.

PSALM 147:3

At my first defense, no one came to my support, but everyone deserted me. May it not be held against them. But the Lord stood at my side and gave me strength.

2 TIMOTHY 4:16-17

"I am with you and will watch over you wherever you go. . . . I will not leave you until I have done what I have promised you."

GENESIS 28:15

"Do not let your hearts be troubled. You believe in God; believe also in me."

JOHN 14:1

Though my father and mother forsake me, the LORD will receive me.

PSALM 27:10

May the Lord of peace himself give you peace at all times and in every way. The Lord be with all of you.

2 THESSALONIANS 3:16

The peace of God, which transcends all understanding, will guard your hearts and your minds in Christ Jesus.

PHILIPPIANS 4:7

Let the **PEACE** of Christ rule in your hearts, since as members of one body you were called to peace. And be thankful. . . . Whatever you do, whether in word or deed, do it all in the name of the Lord Jesus, giving **THANKS** to God the Father through him.

COLOSSIANS 3:15, 17

35

THANK-YOU-NOTE MAN

There has always been something very unusual about Billy Webb. It took me a while to figure out what was so special about this particular friend.

Then one day it hit me. Billy is a handwritten-thank-you-note man. From the very first time we met for lunch until our most recent outing, I've received a note in the mail a few days later from him. These notes are not long and drawn out; in fact, they usually fit on one side of a four-by-six card. But even when he has picked up the tab for lunch, Billy thanks me for my time and for my friendship.

The apostle Paul opened nearly every one of his thirteen New Testament letters with a "thank you." The letter to the church in Philippi is especially strong. "I thank my God every time I remember you. In all my prayers for all of you, I always pray with joy because of your partnership in the gospel," he wrote (Philippians 1:3–5).

Are you a thank-you-note man in the lives of your children, grandchildren, family, and friends? Being such a man takes only a moment, but the dividends are astonishing. Try it. You'll see.

—ROBERT WOLGEMUTH

GOD'S WORDS FOR YOU, GRANDPA

Praise the LORD. Give thanks to the LORD, for he is good; his love endures forever.

PSALM 106:1

I will extol the LORD at all times; his praise will always be on my lips.

PSALM 34:1

By prayer and petition, with thanksgiving, present your requests to God.

PHILIPPIANS 4:6

Thanks be to God, who always leads us as captives in Christ's triumphal procession and uses us to spread the aroma of the knowledge of him everywhere.

2 CORINTHIANS 2:14

Give thanks in all circumstances; for this is God's will for you in Christ Jesus.

1 THESSALONIANS 5:18

Thanks be to God! He gives us the victory through our Lord Jesus Christ.

1 CORINTHIANS 15:57

I will give thanks to the LORD because of his righteousness; I will sing the praises of the name of the LORD Most High.

PSALM 7:17

Just as you received Christ Jesus as Lord, continue to live your lives in him, rooted and built up in him, strengthened in the faith as you were taught, and overflowing with thankfulness.

COLOSSIANS 2:6-7

You turned my wailing into dancing; you removed my sackcloth and clothed me with joy, that my heart may sing your praises and not be silent. LORD my God, I will praise you forever.

PSALM 30:11-12

Let them give thanks to the LORD for his unfailing love and his wonderful deeds for mankind.

PSALM 107:21

Thanks be to God for his indescribable gift!

2 CORINTHIANS 9:15

"The LORD **BLESS** you and keep you;

the LORD make his face shine on you

and be **GRACIOUS** to you;

the LORD turn his face toward you

and give you peace."

NUMBERS 6:24-26

36

MORNING JOY

Roaring winds, the spray of sleet and snow, dangerous and slippery ice. Remember those storms when you were a child? I sure do. I'd shiver under my quilt. Would the house survive? Would I? Moaning winds made me feel lonesome. Would morning ever come?

Yes, but with it, a different picture. I awoke to soft rays of sun warming my bed covers. Quiet called me out of bed and to the window where I gasped at the dazzling white landscape. It was beautiful.

There are days when my soul feels windblown, raw, and exposed—times when I'm tossed in a blustery tempest with everything breaking loose. But the God who brings beauty out of blizzards promises to bring peace after the storm. And when the beauty dawns, I hardly remember the fright of that stormy trial.

If you sense storm warnings, hold on to a couple of "winter watch" verses from Scripture. Recall how near and present the Lord really is. Remember that joy comes in the morning. Let Him cover your fear with His love, like a blanket of snow, soft and gentle. Cling to His promise of peace.

—JONI EARECKSON TADA

GOD'S WORDS FOR YOU, GRANDPA

"Peace I leave with you; my peace I give you. I do not give to you as the world gives. Do not let your hearts be troubled and do not be afraid."

JOHN 14:27

In peace I will lie down and sleep, for you alone, LORD, make me dwell in safety.

PSALM 4:8

LORD, you establish peace for us; all that we have accomplished you have done for us.

ISAIAH 26:12

Grace and peace to you from God our Father and the Lord Jesus Christ.

PHILIPPIANS 1:2

You will keep in perfect peace those whose minds are steadfast, because they trust in you.

ISAIAH 26:3

The fruit of that righteousness will be peace; its effect will be quietness and confidence forever.

ISAIAH 32:17

Strive for full restoration, encourage one another, be of one mind, live in peace. And the God of love and peace will be with you.

2 CORINTHIANS 13:11

When the LORD takes pleasure in anyone's way, he causes their enemies to make peace with them.

PROVERBS 16:7

Seek peace and pursue it.

PSALM 34:14

Great peace have those who love your law, and nothing can make them stumble.

PSALM 119:165

He came and preached peace to you who were far away and peace to those who were near. For through him we both have access to the Father by one Spirit.

EPHESIANS 2:17-18

"Everyone who hears these words of mine and puts them into **PRACTICE** is like a wise man who built his house on the rock. The rain came down, the **STREAMS** rose, and the winds blew and beat against that house; yet it did not fall, because it had its **FOUNDATION** on the rock."

MATTHEW 7:24–25

37

STANDING APPOINTMENT

E very day the young president of an East Coast company instructed his secretary not to disturb him, because he had an important appointment.

One morning the chairman of the board arrived unannounced and said, "I want to see Mr. Jones."

The secretary answered, "I'm sorry. He cannot be disturbed. He has an important appointment."

The chairman became angry and banged open the door. Upon seeing the president of the corporation on his knees in prayer, the chairman quietly backed out of the office and softly closed the door. He asked the secretary, "Is that usual?"

When she answered, "Yes, sir. Every morning," the chairman replied, "No wonder we come to him for advice."

This company president offers each of us a good example.

Do you make a regular appointment with God each day—and do you keep it?

And when you meet with your Father, is a request for wisdom for your day part of the conversation?

—BILLY GRAHAM

GOD'S WORDS FOR YOU, GRANDPA

I instruct you in the way of wisdom and lead you along straight paths. When you walk, your steps will not be hampered; when you run, you will not stumble.

PROVERBS 4:11–12

The wisdom that comes from heaven is first of all pure; then peace-loving, considerate, submissive, full of mercy and good fruit, impartial and sincere.

JAMES 3:17

I will instruct you and teach you in the way you should go; I will counsel you with my loving eye on you.

PSALM 32:8

Whether you turn to the right or to the left, your ears will hear a voice behind you, saying, "This is the way; walk in it."

ISAIAH 30:21

Know also that wisdom is like honey for you: If you find it, there is a future hope for you, and your hope will not be cut off.

PROVERBS 24:14

Get wisdom, get understanding; do not forget my words or turn away from them. Do not forsake wisdom, and she will protect you; love her, and she will watch over you. The beginning of wisdom is this: Get wisdom. Though it cost all you have, get understanding.

PROVERBS 4:5-7

In all your ways submit to him, and he will make your paths straight. Do not be wise in your own eyes; fear the LORD and shun evil. This will bring health to your body and nourishment to your bones.

PROVERBS 3:6-8

Do you not know? Have you not heard? The LORD is the everlasting God, the Creator of the ends of the earth. He will not grow tired or weary, and his understanding no one can fathom.

ISAIAH 40:28

My son, pay attention to my wisdom, turn your ear to my words of insight, that you may maintain discretion and your lips may preserve knowledge.

PROVERBS 5:1-2

If any of you lacks wisdom, you should ask God, who gives generously to all without finding fault, and it will be given to you.

JAMES 1:5

"Let the **BELOVED** of the

LORD rest secure in him,

for he shields him all day long,

and the one the LORD loves **RESTS**

between his shoulders."

DEUTERONOMY 33:12

38
PERFECT REST

I knew a Christian lady who had a very heavy temporal burden. One day, she noticed a little tract called "Anna's Faith." She picked it up and began to read it. The story was of a poor woman who had been carried triumphantly through a life of unusual sorrow. She was giving the history of her life to a kind visitor, and the visitor said feelingly, "Oh, Anna, I do not see how you could bear so much sorrow!"

"I did not bear it," was the quick reply. "The Lord bore it for me."

"Yes," said the visitor, "that is the right way. We must take our troubles to the Lord."

"Yes," replied Anna, "but we must do more than that: we must leave them there. Most people take their burdens to Him, but they bring them away with them again. But I take mine and I leave them with Him, and come away and forget them. If the worry comes back, I take it to Him again; and I do this over and over, until at last I just forget I have any worries and am at perfect rest."

—Hannah Whitall Smith

GOD'S WORDS FOR YOU, GRANDPA

"Come to me, all you who are weary and burdened, and I will give you rest. Take my yoke upon you and learn from me, for I am gentle and humble in heart, and you will find rest for your souls."

MATTHEW 11:28-29

The LORD replied, "My Presence will go with you, and I will give you rest."

EXODUS 33:14

Whoever dwells in the shelter of the Most High will rest in the shadow of the Almighty.

PSALM 91:1

This is what the LORD says: "Stand at the crossroads and look; ask for the ancient paths, ask where the good way is, and walk in it, and you will find rest for your souls."

JEREMIAH 6:16

Return to your rest, my soul, for the LORD has been good to you.

PSALM 116:7

"I will refresh the weary and satisfy the faint."

JEREMIAH 31:25

He makes me lie down in green pastures, he leads me beside quiet waters, he refreshes my soul. He guides me along the right paths for his name's sake.

PSALM 23:2–3

Because so many people were coming and going that they did not even have a chance to eat, [Jesus] said to them, "Come with me by yourselves to a quiet place and get some rest."

MARK 6:31

You know the message God sent to the people of Israel, announcing the good news of peace through Jesus Christ, who is Lord of all.

ACTS 10:36

"Be sure to fear the LORD and serve him **FAITHFULLY** with all your heart; consider what **GREAT** things he has done for you."

1 SAMUEL 12:24

39

SERVE WITH JOY

Delight in God's service is a sign of His acceptance. Those who serve God with a sad face because what they are doing is unpleasant are not serving Him. They are bringing a form of homage, but life is absent.

God does not require slaves to grace His throne. He is Lord of the empire of love and His servants dress in robes of joy. The angels of God serve with songs, not with groans. Just a murmur or a sigh would be mutiny because obedience that is not voluntary is disobedience. The Lord looks at the heart, and if we were forced to serve, He would reject our offering. Service coupled with joy is heart service, and heart service is true service.

"The joy of the LORD is your strength" (Nehemiah 8:10). Joy removes difficulties. Joy is to our service as oil is to the wheels of a railroad car. Without oil the axle grows hot and accidents occur. If there is no holy joy to oil our wheels, our spirit will soon be clogged with weariness.

Let me ask you a question. Do you serve the Lord with joy? Then show the people of the world, who think our religion is slavery, that serving God is a delight and a joy.

—CHARLES H. SPURGEON

GOD'S WORDS FOR YOU, GRANDPA

Have the same mindset as Christ Jesus: Who, being in very nature God, did not consider equality with God something to be used to his own advantage; rather, he made himself nothing by taking the very nature of a servant, being made in human likeness. And being found in appearance as a man, he humbled himself by becoming obedient to death—even death on a cross!

PHILIPPIANS 2:5-8

Serve one another humbly in love.

GALATIANS 5:13

Though I am free and belong to no one, I have made myself a slave to everyone, to win as many as possible. To the Jews I became like a Jew, to win the Jews. To those under the law I became like one under the law (though I myself am not under the law), so as to win those under the law. To those not having the law I became like one not having the law (though I am not free from God's law but am under Christ's law), so as to win those not having the law. To the weak I became weak, to win the weak. I have become all things to all people so that by all possible means I might save some.

1 CORINTHIANS 9:19-22

Serve wholeheartedly, as if you were serving the Lord, not people, because you know that the Lord will reward each one for whatever good they do.

EPHESIANS 6:7–8

We have different gifts, according to the grace given to each of us. If your gift is prophesying, then prophesy in accordance with your faith; if it is serving, then serve; if it is teaching, then teach.

ROMANS 12:6–7

"Now that I, your Lord and Teacher, have washed your feet, you also should wash one another's feet. I have set you an example that you should do as I have done for you."

JOHN 13:14–15

"Whoever welcomes this little child in my name welcomes me; and whoever welcomes me welcomes the one who sent me. For it is the one who is least among you all who is the greatest."

LUKE 9:48

I will extol the LORD with all my heart in the council of the upright and in the assembly. Great are the works of the LORD; they are pondered by all who delight in them.

PSALM 111:1–2

We continually ask God . . . that you may live a life **WORTHY** of the Lord and please him in every way: bearing fruit in every good work, **GROWING** in the knowledge of God, being strengthened with all power according to his glorious might so that you may have great **ENDURANCE** and patience.

COLOSSIANS 1:9–11

160

40

THE LORD REJOICES

Strength is an inside secret. It comes from the Lord's Spirit in the well of our inner being. Because His strength is limitless, our wells need never be empty. His strength is constantly surging up to give us exactly what we need in every moment.

Zephaniah gives the secret of lasting strength. Note the glorious progression in Zephaniah 3:17: "The LORD your God is with you, the Mighty Warrior who saves. He will take great delight in you; in his love he will no longer rebuke you, but will rejoice over you with singing." First, the Lord takes great delight in you. In spite of all our failures, He has chosen to be our God and to cherish us. Think of it! This gives us the confidence of strength. We belong to God—He's redeemed us in Christ and placed His Spirit in us. He'll never give up on us.

Next, the Lord quiets us with His love. The unqualified, indefatigable love of the Lord gives us confidence, security, and peace. There's no need to prove ourselves or blow our own horns. We can live with calm, winsome joy. And knowing that the Lord rejoices over us frees us to rejoice in Him.

—LLOYD JOHN OGILVIE

GOD'S WORDS FOR YOU, GRANDPA

The LORD gives strength to his people; the LORD blesses his people with peace.

PSALM 29:11

"I will strengthen them in the LORD and in his name they will live securely," declares the LORD.

ZECHARIAH 10:12

He said to me, "My grace is sufficient for you, for my power is made perfect in weakness." Therefore I will boast all the more gladly about my weaknesses, so that Christ's power may rest on me. That is why, for Christ's sake, I delight in weaknesses, in insults, in hardships, in persecutions, in difficulties. For when I am weak, then I am strong.

2 CORINTHIANS 12:9-10

The LORD is the strength of his people, a fortress of salvation for his anointed one.

PSALM 28:8

"In the LORD alone are deliverance and strength."

ISAIAH 45:24

Strengthen me according to your word.

PSALM 119:28

"Wealth and honor come from you; you are the ruler of all things. In your hands are strength and power to exalt and give strength to all."

1 CHRONICLES 29:12

I pray that out of his glorious riches he may strengthen you with power through his Spirit in your inner being.

EPHESIANS 3:16

I can do all this through him who gives me strength.

PHILIPPIANS 4:13

Enter his gates with thanksgiving and his courts with praise; give thanks to him and praise his name.

PSALM 100:4

Come, let us sing for joy to the LORD; let us shout aloud to the Rock of our salvation. Let us come before him with thanksgiving and extol him with music and song.

PSALM 95:1–2

BIBLIOGRAPHY

All excerpts used by permission. Italics in Scripture indicate the author's emphasis.

Arthur, Kay. *Beloved: From God's Heart to Yours: A Daily Devotional*. Harvest House, 1994.

Eppinga, Jacob D. *As Long As I Live: Thoughts on Growing Older*. Faith Alive Christian Resources, 1993.

Gilhuis, Cornelis. *Conversations on Growing Older*. William B. Eerdmans, 1977.

God Is Faithful: MyDaily® Devotional. Thomas Nelson, 2014.

Graham, Billy. *Where I Am: Heaven, Eternity, and Our Life Beyond*. Thomas Nelson, 2015.

Graham, Billy. *Wisdom for Each Day*. Thomas Nelson, 2008.

Jeremiah, Dr. David. *Ever Faithful: A 365-Day Devotional*. Thomas Nelson, 2018.

Jeremiah, Dr. David. *Morning and Evening Devotions Holy Moments in the Presence of God*. Thomas Nelson, 2017.

Lucado, Max. *Before Amen: The Power of a Simple Prayer*. Thomas Nelson, 2014.

Lucado, Max, *A Gentle Thunder*. Word, 1995.

Lucado, Max. *On the Anvil: Stories on Being Shaped into God's Image*. Thomas Nelson, 1994.

MacArthur, John. *Drawing Near: Daily Readings for a Deeper Faith*. Crossway Books, 1993.

Manning, Brennan. *Abba's Child: The Cry of the Heart for Intimate Belonging*. NavPress, 1994.

Maxwell, John C. and Jim Dornan. *Becoming a Person of Influence: How to Positively Influence the Lives of Others*. Thomas Nelson, 1997.

Mom's Devotional Bible. With devotions by Elisa Morgan. Zondervan, 1996.

Morgan, Robert J. *Always Near: 10 Ways to Delight in the Closeness of God*. Thomas Nelson, 2019.

Nouwen, Henri J. M. *Our Greatest Gift: A Meditation on Dying and Caring*. HarperCollins, 1994.

Ogilvie, Lloyd John. *Silent Strength: God's Wisdom for Daily Living*. Harvest House, 1990.

Sanders, J. Oswald. *Enjoying Your Best Years: Staying Young While Growing Older*. Discovery House, 1993.

Schuller, Robert H. *A Walk of Faith: Living Positively One Day at a Time*. Robert Schuller Ministries, 1985.

Shaw, Jean. *The Better Half of Life: Meditations from Ecclesiastes*. Zondervan, 1983.

Smith, Hannah Whitall. *The Christian's Secret of a Happy Life*. 1875.

Stafford, Tim. *As Our Years Increase: Answers to Questions About Retirement, Finances, Health, Changing Relationships, Death.* InterVarsity Press, 1992.

Stoop, Jan and Betty Southard. *The Grandmother Book: Sharing Your Special Joys and Gifts with a New Generation.* Thomas Nelson, 1993.

Swindoll, Charles R. *Laugh Again.* Thomas Nelson, 1992.

Tada, Joni Eareckson. *Diamonds in the Dust: 366 Sparkling Devotions.* Zondervan, 1993.

The Devotional Bible for Dads. With notes by Robert Wolgemuth. Zondervan, 1999.

FAVORITE MEMORIES

....

....

....

....

....

....

....

....

....

....

....

FAVORITE MEMORIES

....

....

....

....

....

....

....

....

....

....

....

....

FAVORITE MEMORIES

FAVORITE MEMORIES